forged
in
FIRE

held
in
love

forged in FIRE | held in *love*

A Collection Written By:

Nomad the Poet

MAMA'S KITCHEN PRESS

forged in fire, held in love
© 2024, NOMAD the Poet
ISBN (paperback): 979-8-9853373-7-2

Published by Mama's Kitchen Press
Austin, TX / Los Angeles, CA
mamaskitchenpress.com

First Trade Paperback Original Edition, 2024

Printed in the United States of America

Cover Illustration by Luke Buenaventura
Cover Design by Luke Buenaventura
Edited by Anne Marie Wells and Camari Carter Hawkins
Layout Design by Luke Buenaventura

dedication

Luke—

Your love has given Me the freedom to explore, the bravery to LOVE, and the inspiration to C R E A T E.
thank you for all that You are.

Thank you for holding space for me, my wild and my tender. Your support on this journey is a blessing.

xx

For My Love, My Family, and My Inner Child...may She forever run in the pastures I've laid for Her.

acknowledgements

To my chosen family,

Thank you.

Thank you for providing a soft landing ground through the storm. Thank you for your support, your love, your authentic selves, and your belief in me.

To Alex Petunia, thank you for your gentle guidance. To Ruddy, my CLI family, and my incredible team at Mama's Kitchen Press: you gave me structure, you gave me insight, you encouraged me to continue the birthing cycle of this book, and I thank you deeply.

To my mother,
Thank you for doing your best and lifting me up onto your shoulders. Thank you for the love, support, and nurturing my voice through the stories we'd create around the dinner table. The path you forged, unknowingly, gave me direction and clarity for my own—

I hope you know that.

table of contents

part i

row 26E

depression hits subtly

of the poular tree

4C

888

meditate

ocean's baptism

part ii

dancing shadows

how healing feels

on black beauty

the sable dragonfly

a message from Spirit, calling to me

praise

communion

the birth of venus

afrodite rising

the story of the wasp, as told by the wasp to its fig

the story of the fig, as told by the fig to its wasp

this is what healing looks like

part iii

held in love

how healing blooms

fern gully

jupiter rising

an anniversary at trick–or–treat plantation trail

culver city

chiquita

that one summer we only listened to frank ocean

sable

i – a mantra

burbank

kauai

wanderlust

yosemite

monsoon

foreword

by, Alex Petunia

Author, *Tending My Wild*

Literary heroes like Nomad the Poet immerse themselves deep into the embers of human existence – walking fiercely through the flames of trauma, the fires of fear, the blazes of injustice. This ruthless heat may ravage a person into forgotten ash, but it never devours Nomad the Poet. Instead, she emerges from the wildfire chaos with a burning tongue of power. With a torch called pen and a might called heart, she fuels her own pathway toward healing, loving, and flourishing in this debut poetry collection *Forged in Fire, Held in Love*. This collection embodies her resilient march through the hellfires of life with a relentless dedication to deepening purpose, an immense commitment to craft and a loving devotion to soul–sparking the awe within us.

I had the privilege of working with Nomad the Poet as her Community Literature Initiative guide. I've witnessed her tender adoration for self and an elevating grace as she navigated all angles of building this manuscript. As we evaluated her poems line by line, I understood her to be a poet seeking an authentic expression of healing as liberation. Every period, every comma, every capital, every moment of bold or italics, every intricate aspect of this collection was compiled with meticulous attention rooted in a conscientious connection to the readers' experience with her words. I am truly honored to witness Nomad the Poet ascend beyond the ashes of ache toward her path of superbloom. I've been moved by the seeds of hope she has sprinkled into every stanza and the intention put into every page. I've watched in real time how she transforms the scorch of torment into a setting sun of shimmering gratitude. Nomad the Poet is a writer who has lived through the scars of rebirth, not as a phoenix rising but something even more profound — a human bravely erupting and boldly thriving. Her poetry shifts vulnerabilities into a creative courage that often leaves readers awestruck and hopeful in their own healing ascension.

While this world sets itself ablaze, *Forged in Fire, Held in Love* engulfs the reader into a sacred alchemy of wordsmith wisdom, interwoven with awakening affirmations. These poems invite us to swim in stillness, breathe more deeply, and reflect inwardly with self–compassion. This collection is an empowering love force unafraid to excavate the secrets of the past that are yearning for acknowledgement so that healing can begin. This book redefines how we nurture the body, mind, and spirit and shifts pain into purpose into power into perseverance. *Forged in Fire, Held in Love* reminds us that we can find the pathway to our own bloom if we first embrace the ashes of our truths.

Alex Petunia
Community Literature Initiative Faculty
Author, *Tending My Wild*

preface

Hello reader, welcome friend. Thank you for picking up this collection of love and healing. Thank you for taking the time to make this journey with me...we've been waiting for you.

Your presence is a blessing — here and everywhere that you take up space.

This collection was *forged through fire and held in love.* This collection is a rebirth of self, after the fires of life & grief cleansed my palette, providing me new space to cultivate. It is a reckoning and a harvesting. Take good care while reading; take good care while living.

I wrote these poems to anchor myself in the storm; if you are needing encouragement, hope and love, read on. If you are looking for validation, empathy and understanding, read on. The best time to read these words are: when you're seeking, when you're lost, when you're found, when you're open and ready to receive. Journey with me as I move through and break from the uncomfortable, compact soil and spring up a blossoming plumeria.

The best way to read these words: aloud.
Whispered to yourself, read once, then twice,
then three times if that is what you need.

A few aspects of the book that would behoove you to pay attention to:

Selah	In the Bible, Selah, appears in Psalms, a book of songs and worship. The word indicates to the reader and instruments playing to pause in silence.

When you see *Selah* please take a moment.

P A U S E

Take a deep inhale in.

R E F L E C T

Do not read on.

Though uncomfortable, I encourage you to sit.
To feel. To be.
Sit in any and all the emotions that may have been brought up.

When you're ready, continue.

As all healing journeys are, this one is uniquely and authentically its own. These poems roll through the valleys and climb the mountains of Life – *My Life.*

Showing the rise, the fall, the pause, and the rise again. I have risen many times, and I will continue to rise.

My prayer is that these words support you in your rise to whatever mountainside you find yourself at.

I hope these words are friends to you, as they have been for me. That they hold you, mirror you, and understand you.

Selah

**With as much love and light one can muster –
NOMAD the Poet**

forged | held
in | in
FIRE | *love*

part i

when

fire

R
E
I
G
N
S

how healing starts...

black girl magic

as i swim in the celestial pools
that reside within my hoops,
i pluck an unsaid prayer
from my teeth.

it talks of the love
that's embedded deep
within my skin,
the wisdom that is caught
between my kinks.

sings the praises of the
meadows that reside,
where my thighs divide.

calls my fields sacred ground-

where both men,
and earth
collide.

Laments,

to the painting of my bones
a deep and vicious red-

the color of the diaspora
that my People have bled.

whispers the longings
of both saint and sinner,

how they confess they
desire my temple
be their next conquest.

how they pray late at night
to swim with their Divine.
ignorant to the light
that lies behind
My eyes

lighthouse ghost stories

i. *sins of the father*

you plucked me from the ground,
held me in your hands.
you tied your secret prayers
to me,
to cast in the ocean;

another penny in your fountain.

placed in my new home
below the light and the waves,
you hoped that
from my sacrifice,
your wish would survive.

joseph,

Selah

like a ship that's docked at port
for a period of time,
you

like a ship at port waiting
for the tide to be deemed clear,
you

Selah

like the port
left alone longing
for the ship's return,

me.

untitled iv.

with each i n h a l e of myself
i exhale a piece of   y

                              o

                                      ↻

                                          •

**a reminder for
later**

a fire grows simply
because we give it the space
to burn.

am
  i
    allowing
myself

s   p   a   c   e
to
        burn?

track 5,
to pimp a butterfly*

if these *walls* could talk.
        if these walls could talk
                if these walls could **talk**...

        they'd bemoan the first time
                a man touched me:

        i was an age
        where numbers were symbols,
        sounds, unknown to my mind.
        gigantic -

                        hands
        chapped from the trauma
        his father afflicted,
        with no salve but
        an ABV percentage
        of 40 or higher
        to comfort
        his night terrors.
        gigantic -

hands, who communed
in the same way
with my mother,
to create the seed
from which I sprouted,
chose to *steal* my innocence
as a sacrifice for his suffering;
wasting into the
generational traumas
our ancestors
prayed for him to heal.
instead–

he polluted the soil in my garden,
ripped out potential and
ejaculated my grandfather's trauma
onto my face.
my chest,
my bed.

if these walls could talk…

they'd censure the second time
        a man touched me:

tricked into a room
under false pretenses,
on the eve of a great aunt's
funeral and my 10th birthday,

let's grab the xbox, i have
a new game to show you.

Happy Birthday

family ties
into trauma and trauma ties
into the family,

his hands were laden
with a white man's greed
that sold him off
centuries ago,
and dehumanized
his women after. so,
it doesn't surprise me
that - i was left,
face down
in shame
while he left,
satisfied.

if
    these
        walls
           could
                talk...

they'd cringe at the third time
    a man touched me:

too timid, too terrified,
too trifling and tone-deaf.
he made up for his shortcomings by
driving me around Los Angeles
in busted cars,
first Bertha,
then Sally.

we'd sing with abandon
on our way to
tequila slicked dance floors.
our only refuge
in a cage of anxiety and
sexuality, confusions and
exploration.

i have your love now,
    but i'd be so lucky to love you
        in five years time.

just   *give me*   *time.*

he couldn't love me
the way i needed
nor could he lose the love
he was receiving, so
he toyed with my emotions
in a five hundred, twenty-five
thousand, six hundred minute
times 3 cat and mouse chase.

if these walls could   T A L K

they'd smile at the first time
       a woman touched me,

made out as an enemy of state
by the men that came before her,
my hands dug out the muck and mire
of my soul to find
the honeysuckle dandelions
of serenity within her,
Me.

her fingers danced
along my skin,
connecting scar lines to
paint an abstract masterpiece.

discomfort became tranquility
after pain relinquished
its cruelty.
        Healing,
with her, i began healing.
with her, i learned releasing.

if these W A L L S could T A L K

they'd laugh with delight
from the fourth man
who touched me.

the last man
who will ever touch me.

they'd sing the psalms I've
transcribed in the twilight hour;
written to the rhythm of his
resting heart rate,
sleeping next to Mine.
bless His hands and
breathe relief because

His divine masculine –
fluid,   gentle   and   strong, met

My divine feminine –
fluid,   graceful   and   resilient.

in a moment greater
than passion,
a moment deeper
than lust,
a moment of collision, after
a decade's long gravitational pull
that led to our souls' inevitable
amalgamation in the concert hall
          of praise.

We   found   love

He came to Me,
as an unexpected consequence of
EMDR and ashanti breaths.
He came to Me,
as a friend of a friend
who grew into a home.
He came to Me,
as an angel number - 11:11
a reminder of the work manifested.

His hands,
release binds that cramp
My vertebrae.
His tongue,
a gentle balm
to the past torments.

His body,
tames the wild that flares
in the night.

if
these
walls
could
talk...

they'd tell the world
that healing is possible,
that the kindling of
a broken past
can breathe *Life*

to the warmest fire,
an everlasting flame.
that the flame can become a hearth
and the hearth can bring purpose.

they'd encourage the hurting –
the broken, the lost, the meek.
tell them my story
for I am a *prophet for healing*.

IF THESE WALLS COULD TALK

Selah.

lineage

there is a mother in this body—
somewhere deep in the marrow,
underneath the shedding of
skin and teeth.
there is a mother
in this body.

there is a mother
in me.

there is a mother
in these teachings—
scrolls cataloged,
collecting fragments
into stories,
buried in the library
of my being.

her voice rings out, echoing,
memories dancing along
the thin line of comfort
and haunting: her tone
etches cursive love notes,
births cognitions—positive,
neutral, negative,
some of them

generations old,
not even her own. so,

she sips cabernet
while listening to
herbie hancock.
she dances through tradition,
elbows deep in flour and dough
as we spend time in the kitchen.
there is a mother
in these teachings,
for my mother's voice
lives eternal in me.

she is one of the oracle,
a griot,
a spoken history book.
she imparts
the sacred wisdom passed down,
over recipes too good
to be written,
so, instead, we cook.

she brings my past
around the flame
to remind me that
family
means
                    forgiveness,

her kneading hands demonstrate
the tension and deterioration
that comes from the forcing
of a malleable creation
into a shape;
unauthentic to their existence,
so, instead she releases
to show me i can, too.

our hands - the defender,
the nurturer -
looms that weave new tapestries,
mirrored lifelines, and
palm signs.
these hands bring forth
the miracles of the divine.

her hands that are my hands
are frozen in time. borrowed,
from her mother,
my hands are on loan
until the next daughter comes
into fruition-
sacred, malleable, and perfect
in size.

there is a mother in this body,
for my future daughter lives
nestled inside of me.

experiencing my life choices
through the emotions i choose
to hold onto.
through her time in the womb,
she learns of the things
I am not strong enough
to let go, but hopefully, soon.

she will carry this weight
that i carry,
but in a different way,
cuz just like my mother,
i will fight
the more terrifying demons
to give her life more ease
through faith.

she will become
whatever life and her journey
need her to be
until one day,
she has the revelation
of the mother in her body,
through the lineage alive
and the mother in me.

death becomes Her

death becomes the Earth
as the phoenix becomes the ash.

a friend, hot
in flames — we'll rise again,
so show me the way home.
take me home.
to the dirt, to the leaves,
to the transformation
back into the trees,
where energy multiples – peace.
Serenity,
you will take me home.
like *Joanne and Saudia,*
Sophie and Grandmother.
show me,
gentle lover, show me —
the truth of darkness,
our meeting ground,
an accession in stardust,
no longer feared,
for they have paved
the way for us.

as death becomes the Earth
like the phoenix becomes the ash.

my vena cava

you've carried me out of the
trenches of Death,
my heartbeat is strong.

you've lead me through
unknown lands
where fear transformed
into prosperity;
my heartbeat is strong.

you've strengthened Our chambers —
weaving tapestries of creation
and resilience
from hate and confusion.
my heartbeat is strong.

each beat — a prophecy,
predicated from my Ancestors' tombs.
each beat — a new legacy,
bred from my Ancestors wounds.

my blood made into wine
with each defiant fist
they held high,
a revolution not televised,
but organized in church rooms.

my heartbeat is strong.

for long distance lovers

a star cannot be of the earth
despite her prayers,
despite how she longs to be.

she cannot kiss the dirt -
her lips were not intended
to graze the dust.

the earth cannot touch her face -
his hands were not made to reach
beyond the heavens.

yet during the twilight hour,
shielded by moonlight,
underneath the cascading shadows
of their gatekeeper,
together-

They pray.

**overlooking the hurricane
that once threatened
my existence**

i. *eye of the hurricane*

as i battle
an invisible current
upstream,
i take deeper breaths
to ensure my survival
from: category 5,
1,095 miles per hour gusts
of life, eroding the remnants of
who i was: she crumbles
into sediments,
becoming fossil artifacts
later to be categorized as:
Nostalgia.

ii. *spiritual warfare*

i've been sleeping on a
spiritual air mattress,

in borrowed rooms
and office spaces,
discovering the word *home*
through mirror reflections and
shadow work.
finding balance in the warfare
on faith and resilience;
what doesn't kill me
manifests in knots so deep,
it scares the chiropractor
every time he touches
me.

iii. *comfortable*

but here,
my love, here
nestled in this interchangeable
spoon under silk sheets
held in your arms,
grounded in your breath,
my roots hold firm on the
foundations
of growth.

they reach up
towards the light of Us,
of You,
a star that rivals the sun,
You.

here — i find the strength
again to continue.
here,
my Love, here

i release on an eight count
Life's humbling hurricanes,
Life's brutal gales,
that have swelled my lungs
and bruised my chest
for so long,
i almost believed
them a part of my anatomy.
here,
my Love, here,
i don't need to battle
an invisible current
upstream because,

here,
together
we glide on the currents
with wings made of love,
above the bullshit,
all the way up to the stratosphere
and smile.
we s m i l e
'cuz we now
overlook the hurricane
that once threatened my existence.

compromise

bless these hands

a gentle kiss
beneath a hazy new moon
as a white flag,
we find our way back to romance

these hands are magic.

we're finding our way back
to the beginning days;
like when our rental car's flat
stopped us in the middle of a
barren spring desert.

i feel the most vulnerable,
right now with you.

selah

#melaninrich:
an ode to police officers

This Ain't Yo Mamma's Civil Rights
Movement

This Is Me Claiming My Black Body
Back Movement
Me Unapologetically
Taking Up
              Space
                        Movement.

This Ain't Your Daddy's Daddy's
Negro Saying
              "Yessir"
                    "Nosir"
    *"I'll Hang My Head Below Yours
Sir"* Movement.

This Is: I Will Not Go Silently In
The Night Movement.

This Is: How Are You Going To Tell
Me The Police Shootings That

Pop!
Pop!
Pop!

Every Other Night
Ain't The New Strange Fruit
Movement?

I Dare You To **Look At Me.**
I Dare You To See ***A Black Woman,***
A Human Being.

Breathing and Loving,
Hurting and Learning,
Living.

I Dare You To Not
Hypersexualize Me

I'm Going To Say It Again...

I Dare You Not
To Hypersexulaize Me.

I Dare You To See Me Throw Up
My Hands In Heavenly Worship,
Not At The Barrel Of *Your Gun*
With *My Hands Up*,
Praying You **Don't Shoot.**

I Dare You To Go Against The
Images Of People Who Look Like Me.
The Images That The Man
Controlling The Strings
Has Poisoned Your Mind With.

I Demand You To Listen To Me.
Listen To My Mind, To My Voice.
I Demand That You ***Respect Me.***
Don't Tell Me That I'm Articulate.
Don't Tell Me That What I Have To
Say Is Cute.

I Demand Excellence,

From My Country,
My Government.
I Demand Excellence From My Elders
And My Peers.
I Demand Excellence From Myself.

**This Ain't Your Mamma's Civil
Rights Movement.**

rainbow cover,
black spine

my skin is the hue
of Blue, royal,
deep and full.
signifying the blood
in my veins from
the Kings and Queens
i descend from.

my hair is a luscious Green,
the color of our Mother
before Man defiled her,
ever-growing and wild,
untamed and soft,
with hidden secrets and mirth.

my eyes bear a Golden glow,
luminescent and beautiful,
timeless and strained.
shining the lights of
Heaven to illuminate the night.

my spine is a beaten
Black,

muddied,
bruised,
blocked…
tender to the touch
with footprint tattoos
that decorate my decaying
vertebra.
grazed with the scraps of
Progression...

all lives matter
until you're the latter

Black and **Female**

but my skin is the shade of
royalty,
my hair, the shade of nature,
my eyes are the sun,
and i'm still standing,
lifting You up.

family tree

to find Me,
i had to lose You.

Selah

lose my understanding
of self:
within the dynamic of
You, the dynamic of us,
of who i once was
and was told to be -

family...

Selah

i uprooted the foundation
of our family tree,
finding, decaying
six feet below me,
a malnourished graveyard -

our family legacy.

Selah

I cried.
You screamed.
I was silent.
You turned away...
but healing happened-

as I chose to till new soil
into boundaries,
healing happened.
as I began to root,
breaking through
the compacted earth
of myself-
healing happened.

as I shattered each
generational chain that
was rusted over from neglect,
healing happened.
as I chose to nurture
my sapling heart,
blooming maturely,
on a stronger foundation
of worth and truth-
healing happened.

though You
felt I abandoned You,

healing happened.

Selah.

then Love came.
and *that* remains.

pcs: please consider sympathy

after the third cat scan and
second visit to the ER,
eighth month of flare ups,
headaches and debilitation,
they finally gave me a name
to call the shadow:
"you have
Post Concussive Syndrome"

•

dearest one,
you will feel pain -
you will traverse the
lands on a journey
to heal, to find that the
sunrise simply settles
at the summit
of your chest.

you will forget your capacity.
your inner voice will briefly
be silenced by the thunderous
roar from the mouths of
capitalism,

fed by the ableist,
sexist, and racist
dogma that devours
others to fuel it.

and, in the cleansing
of the rains –
life's funny hurricanes,
you'll find yourself dancing
in between the raindrops.

yes, my love,
you will dance again.
a freshly sprouted vine
nourished by the Mother's
love, drenched and finding
peace within the whirlwinds.
it will take you **years**
before you truly understand –
the rain is your friend,
the typhoon, your caretaker.

you will find yourself
relearning to walk,
a humbling encounter
behind the backdrops
of hospital rooms, physical
therapy and speech pathology.

be gentle, please,
for as you navigate
this rebirth
you will lose
almost _everything_
but gain deep:
understanding, humanity,
wisdom, capacity.
money comes, goes
and comes again,

the definition of family
will evolve and change,
but the character developed
in this hardship

is the unalienable
framework for,

_ME._
authenticity,
purpose,
identity -
so, as you dig deep
to discover
the beauty in this
pilgrimage, please,
consider sympathy.

chronic

who's gonna tell you to move
when the weight in your chest
pushes you to the bottom
of the currents?
pitch black around you,

the ocean whispers,
"you gotta choose,"

as her waves carry you backward,
then propels you forward,
you catch lessons
in the middle of whiplash…
you wake up and go to work
'cuz bills are due.

This is the cycle,
rinse and repeat with beautiful
moments in between,
your hormones are unbalanced, so,
the earth speaks.
"sweetheart, get you to the trees.
there's no progress without rest,
no revolution without winter — you
can't continue forward without it"
So I *breathe*

in your 20s, healing
looks like losing all of
your friends.

i have outgrown the places where grown people go to escape.

impermanence

everything is temporary,
even this pain
that i hold.

everything is temporary,
even the joy
that'll unfold.

i feel it,
i feel so aligned
with the Divine;
    i see it.
    the road ahead,
    though i know not
    where my feet tread...

everything is temporary.

see you soon...

i said,
"see you soon" to you today...
it wasn't a "goodbye"
just a, "I need some time."
and I thought I'd feel better
after saying it,
but right now i feel
like *shit.*

it's difficult to put into
words how much i love you.
it's difficult to put
into words
how much i love myself.
how much i value
and protect myself,
i know this is the best
for the both of us,
but,

Damn...

i thought healing would
make me feel better, not
make me present enough
to feel the full weight of

Goodbye...

see you soon...
it's see you soon...

i miss you.
but I know right now,
we're not good
for one another.
and i miss you.
and i know right now
you're hurting as well,
and i miss you.
but i know that for any
kind of growth or healing,
or acknowledgment
of what *actually* happened
to come,
i need to say,

"see you soon"...

you surprised me
when you accepted it

without any...
lashing out, any yelling,
any gaslighting,
manipulating,
any kind of emotional
reaction that i've grown
so accustomed to.
and maybe, seeking in
the moment to feel
your love; that's the only
way you've been able to
communicate it, as of late.

so, to be honest,
a part of me wanted the heat,
the extra hurt to add to the
grief, a love sting, a memory...
instead you said, "okay."

said this would be the last time
i'd hear from you
until i was ready
to reach out.
you said "I love you too."
you said "see you soon..."

see you soon...

row 26E

high above the clouds, i feel
connected to the divine.
maybe that's why this depression
i'm moving through
shares thoughts of me dying,
not to escape this life,
but to get a different
perspective, to see
the wonders of this earth,
this homeland, this body.

selah

volcanic magma that fought
through the icy currents of the
sea,
creating life to form land,
beauty over a millennia-
existence in its simplicity.

thank you Spirit, for this reminder
that life is more than the emotions
i move through.
thank you God, for showing me
that there's beauty
in the barren lands, too.

i shared this revelation
with my mother,
that i am moving through
depression, and that it's okay
her immediate thoughts echoed the
generation of the world
that she grew up in.
one that forced her to behave,

thoughts of weakness
reverberated off her tongue,
questions rose of what
and where she went wrong,
because to be a
              black woman
        alive
in america
      is to be "strong."
selah
a quiet like-fire was ignited
in my chest, that fueled
my trembling lips
to give her soul a new perspective:

why do you think my vulnerability
isn't strong?

standing on the foundation
i've been laying,

the past several years
in back-breaking therapy,
I challenged, her,
indoctrinated beliefs:

i can be hurting and resilient.
i can be sad and content.
i trust myself enough to know,
that this too shall pass.
i am enough, and i'll figure out
the rest.
selah

i looked my mom in the eyes
with security and respect,
i told her
i can look myself in the mirror
proud and still be depressed,
and that's okay,

and i'm okay,
and i will be okay.
i affirmed and spoke my truth
until a dam broke from my tongue,
pouring out uncontainable love
for her,
for me,
for this generational curse
being broken as i speak;
going against what it is
to be a **black** *woman*

in this society, and
choosing vulnerability.
my soul's resistance,
simplicity in existence.

like the terrain below the plane
that charged my heart
with a new perspective,
my strength comes from honesty,
my strength comes from hope,
even when there's turbulence,
on the wings of faith
i'll fight like hell
to float.

to be one with the clouds,
above the pressure of the
oxygen we breathe,
is to be in heaven's front row
where the chosen angels
lay to see,
to watch,
to reminisce,
to surrender.

in the limbo above the clouds
i'm reminded to surrender.

selah

depression hits subtly

she's still me.
in the mirror i catch myself
saying,
she's still me.

i'm still breathing.
even though they tried
to steal my breath
to strengthen their spines,
i'm still breathing.

alive.

of the popular tree

a white man called me
a nigger
the other day.

stripped my dignity
and left me for dead,
gasping in the street.
his entitlement hit me
with such an accuracy –
the residue of his ignorance
lingered on my skin for
days.

he could never understand
sitting in his
ivory tower
of skin,
the weight of the word.
how could he?
that word was forged in the belly
of my brothers.

history loitered with
Strange Fruit
from a
strange garden.

plucked by your hands
and wrung out to dry...
yet we're the Cain
to your holy Able,
and the monsters under your bed.

4c

i. they call my hair twisted.
    christening its coils and texture
    distracting,
    as they
    reach out to cop a feel.

    offended at my offense
    as if they haven't
    taken enough.

ii. they tell me straight hair is
    the "new" thing -
    commenting how
    if i'd only follow their beauty
    regimen,
    strand for strand
    how much more beautiful i'd be.
    as if burning out my heritage
    wasn't a travesty.

iii. So, respectfully...
    don't touch my hair
    White man.
    don't touch my hair.

888
the cycle completion

the wait is over
the cycle has been completed
8 carved in a tree,
my sign, that life
will now be filled with ease.
i've been running up everest
with the chains of my ancestors
on my waist.
bearing their sins,
their unfinished work,
their prayers across
metaphorical planes.
chosen to be the chain breaker,
born with a halo and a noose
around my neck,
imperialism and white culture
made strange fruit start
in the womb

selah

my ancestors died before
fulfilling their purpose.

selah

these past 27 years of life
in lessons have shown me
the plans for the future
generations,
the plans- for them-
i'll continue to protect.
god's been telling me
i may not see
the finished fruit,
may not taste
the sweet honey nectar
from the labor i put in
replanting soul roots.
but god's been telling me
that my work is heavenly –

the fabric of my soul divine
blessed with the fight in me,
the fire my kinfolk refined.

i am: the chain breaker,
cycle releaser
abolishing centuries of;
sterilization
colonization
oppression
recession
doubt
fear
depression

releasing hating on my melanin
because a white jesus lied to me
so i would pick cotton- i
am the archangel and warrior
releasing and conquering.
the cycle has been completed,
my brethren.

rejoice, take pause,
respite, and grow.
the cycle has been completed…

how will this new one unfold?

meditate

when i don't have the words
to write,
i sing.
when i start to loose
the melody,
i Breathe.

the anxious thoughts lie
in wait,
bangin' eagerly at heaven's gates.
fear creeps up my spine,
it threatens to silence my shine -
so, i close my eyes,
to count:

1

love is in me.

2

i am worthy.

3

i am supported.

breathe

4

i am abundantly blessed.

5

i am resilient.

6

i speak life and love over me.

7

i am graceful and intentional.

8

i am bigger than the thoughts that try to control me.

9

i am living my best life.

breathe

10

i am protected.

an ocean baptism

inhale.

inhale deeper.

    breathe sis,
    breathe in the salt water
    and exhale their toxins.
    allow life to fester
    in the form
    of coral and pink,
    and become overgrown.

inhale.

inhale deeper.

    wade sis,
    wade in the water
    and let the quagmire
    that has caked itself
    in your ribs,
    be left under the waves
    as you rise anew.

inhale.

inhale deeper.

> know sis,
> know what it is:
> to have this breath
> in your lungs expand
> until you're forced
> to release it.
> that's how you know
> *you're living.*
>
> *live* sis.
> live in the spaces
> they deny you,
> and breathe.
> let them see the beauty
> they are blind to and

breathe.

> take advantage of this day
> that so many of our brethren will
> never see,
> and breathe.

breathe.

breathe.

part ii

dancing

SHADOWS

how healing feels...

i'm good as i am.
if you can't handle me,
it's because i'm too rich for you

on black beauty

the sable dragonfly

ebony rich,
golden skin
feel it pulse
beneath your fingertips.

black body,
crimson night,
how could they understand
your fight?
lifted by royalty,
engulfed in hate,
through your wings
you create —

                    space

                                              y
                              to   *l*
                                    f

oh what beauty you possess,
my sable dragonfly

a message from Spirit, calling to me

the doors have been open,
don't trip now
when walking through.
know you are worthy
know you are deserving,
they opened because
of the power
you have recognized
inside of you.
the power we preordained
for you.

release the chains
of doubt
the blinders
of fear
and depression
allow them to leave
as you enter this new dimension:
27. divine.
the next realm— 9.

it's here,

what you've
been manifesting.

it's here,
what you've
been praying for.
so, claim it.

own it.
be humble,
confident,
and open.

there's more inside,
grander than your mind,
heart, and soul's eye
could have imagined.

it's grander inside,
all of these blessings
are made for you to open
your hand wide
and,

receive.

so, smile,
walk through.

the table is set,
with your loved ones,
even your enemies present
to view,

to see,
to know
what faith looks like
manifested in you.

welcome, love,
we've been expecting you.

praise

there are scriptures burned
into my skin.

late at night, she reads them
aloud.

she brushes her fingers against
the thin sheets of paper,
careful not to tear with
each page turn.

she sings the hymns
other men dare not read.
sings them
aloud,
alone,
until,
the whole room echoes
a hallelujah chorus.

she speaks praises
of me
to those who would listen,
and calls her mission

holy.

she places upon me
an altar,

cold and stone
until she joins me
with warmth –

a smile,
a kiss,
a knowing look and
loving reminder that –
i am whole.

she offers herself,
that of flesh and soul,
in hopes that she is
a worthy sacrifice.

in her
i have
found
sanctuary.

communion
on sistahood

savor in the honeydew
sip in the sweet nectar
that is –
sisterhood
sistahood

take part in the ritual
of curl patterns,
sun soaking and soul holding
sistahood.
the water from
the eternal fountain
that waters my essence,
sistahood.

heart's asleep and souls
wide awake. we met
a lifetime ago,
dancing in the ethereal plane.
took on this life, in our
newly discovered life forms.
we intersected,
we found each other again,
sista,

we found each other again.

come sit in the
shaded meadow,
come lay down,
blanketed by the
wildflower bloom.
get lost with me
on the dirt road
to get found with me
on the paved road,
sista.

she holds the bottle
to collect my tears,
to remind me of the
hardships i've faced,

replenishing my parched
mouth with the tears
she transformed into honeywater.
this is my sister,
that is my friend.

my mirror and my confidant,
her stories sharpen my pen—
a pastor, a sinner,
the counselor,
and the blood. through the holy
practice of communion, our
sistahood fuels the sun.

the birth of venus

lessons from my mother's life

in this **true** story,
it is said that
Mother Venus was born
as a fully grown
        Woman.

fertilized by the
greed and violent egos
of powerful men,
Venus chose to rise in
        Love,

again and again. after all,
what is a Woman without love?
what is a Woman without the awe-
inspiring, world creating,
tide breaking, life changing
power that is
LOVE?

a *Human,*

prone to corruption,
easily misguided, confused and
growth surely stunted.
unable to evolve
without the wise, good lovin'
that only the Woman possess.

but take heed,
as some will see this
as a threat.

they will
police the Woman,
her body,
her mind,
her voice,
her choice.

until the only thing she can
hear late at night
are the projections
of her policers own shadows,
echoing through their policies',
too dark for even them to address.

see, i was taught this truth
as i was birthed
in the foam and the fire.
held in love
by my Mother Venus
as hell surrounded us.

taught to appreciate the
calefaction, growth's
inauguration.
to smile and thank Tenderness
each time She chose to bless
my sweat covered brow,

just as Venus chose to love.
as my Mother chose to love.
so I choose,
to love.

afrodite rising

[Come Home,]

soaked in the Sun's rays,
dipped in lavender and
as soft as Sakura petals.
cocoa butter, moisturized.
Self doubt, neutralized.
This nappy head, realized,
as prince and key.
This smoky topaz templed
Homeland
breathes.

She sheds.
Our septennial ritual –
a rebirth
a homecoming.
a lesson and reminder
of who I once was,
what she learned,
where she stepped and
where i'll leave

find a new pathway…

[To Me.]

the story of
the wasp,

as told by the wasp to its fig

i.

Time;
the constant yet gentle reminder
that i am not yours,
and you are not mine.
but we are of the same flesh,
same name.
Our journeys intersect
through stardust and hurricanes.
and only through
my beautiful passing
can you be fully recognized,
and bloom. you'll bloom
from my ribcage,
feral, ferocious, free.

so grow wild inside me.
i'll nurture
your pollinated life force
as my own sweet return.
and from sacrifice
and fig flowers,
you will metamorphosize
our wings into fruit seeds.

the story of
the fig,
as told by the fig to its wasp.

ii.

    you released me upon the
evergreen pastures of freedom
to roam.
i'm louder now,

noticeably louder, and
prouder, standing taller,
no longer shrinking smaller
because as you passed the baton
to me,
i flew instead of ran.
flew instead of ran.

selah

flew to the island
where we once discovered
honeycombs and hibiscus.
flew beside our love,
our hands intertwining in his -
a holy matrimony in the sand.
my words, ever embellished
and adorned with the jewels

forged from your flames.

selah

a healing journey
entrenched and nurtured
with each pen smudge and
ink stroke.

every late night,
every tear that you cried
placed lovingly
in a bottle - where
they'll swell over
to form the river i'll cross
to meet you in space and time.

we'll meet in space and time.

this is what healing looks like:

questioning every single
step you take,
every single decision
you make, because
the survivalist in you
has been in overdrive,
fight or flight paralyzed,
since the first time
your beautiful soul
was traumatized.

so please,
dear one, please,
give yourself time
to realize this new path
you've embarked on
will not abide to
your ego,
but your **Growth.**

in layman's terms:
healing <u>will</u> hurt.
and it's okay
you'll thrive;
you have withstood worse.

have patience,
this new path you're on
is in the middle of construction
by your own two hands,
while you simultaneously
take steps forward
on the still setting concrete.

no wonder this process
seems prolonged and obsolete.
baby,

you're trying to run
when there's only room
to crawl, and you don't
even trust your feet.

the same two feet
that have carried you
from the mountain to the valley
to ascend the next mountain.
the same two feet
that have defended
your birthright,
their loyalty boundless –

while you still choose to trust
the eyes that don't see you,
the lives that don't
impart in you –

you trust their projections
and view yourself in a
warped perspective.

fighting your heart
and your gut
while your feet *still*
carry you forward,
regardless.

**this is what healing
looks like:**

incessant movement,
painstaking progress
through the doubt,
releasing the dread
to amass, mile by mile,
ten toes down
with a bowed head –
you,

a humbled warrior
in search of mecca,
until one day you look up
to find yourself,
halfway there.

**this is what healing
looks like:**

have faith,
for this course widdles
out the craven. the feeble,
have faith,
for this course will
bring into question
everything
you believe in.
have faith

dear one. please,
have faith.

on the nights your head throbs
from the released rapids
you wept silently,
on the days when the strain
from obligation forces the muscles
in your lungs to concave
into arthritic spasms,
keep faith,
keep hope

keep faith,
keep Love,
ever present, always in view,
She will be your comfort.
keep Her safe, alive,
unrestricted inside of you.

see,

**this is what healing
looks like:**

a perpetual dance
with balance and gratitude;
the understanding that someday,
even if only for a moment,
the discomfort you feel
will renew as contentment
in existence.

how someday
that fleeting moment
of peace
will grow howling and free.

**this is what healing
looks like:**

the journey,
not the destination.
so find the beauty
in the suffering –

Life's most ironic, yet
important teaching.
find the small reprieves
of light
in the dark side of
the mooon of your heart.
the Yin and the Yang
you might think me insane,
but <u>i promise,</u>
once you find
your own unique way to balance
grief and joy,
Life will grant you
more peace amongst the pain.

see,

**this is what healing
looks like:**

You.   Me.   Us.

Selah

part iii

held

in

LVE

how healing blooms...

fern gully

the sweet turbulence of love
guided me to your soul's door.

jupiter rising

i made love to a man
in my mother's necklace
with the mountainside
and stars in view.
he called me
           baby,
i uttered
           divine
for hours upon hours,
like lovers do.

he walks on cascading stardust
downstream,
calls the Mother his home
and the Sky, his soul.
he: breathes Life,
     exhales Time,
     lays in a quiet mind.

i made love
to a man, in my mother's necklace,
on the eve of my solar return.
he brings me joy,
gifts me safety,
and in this moment,
a rebirth has begun.

an anniversary at trick-or-treat plantation trail

i. san bernardino

a star
in the shape of you,
as we meander
the sides of the san
bernardino mountains.

clouds in the shape
of tool, altitude sickness
to accompany
vulnerable encounters.

we made it another year,
we've eclipsed, the shadows
cleared - doubt no longer
lives here.

Love is made,
Love is found, in fresh
air, trees, and honey shops.

stumbling in the dark,
sinking in silt at the
lakeside, we find –
a star in the shape of you.

ii. big bear lake

grow me in the riverbed
where we filled our canisters
with creekwater.
like your hand as it gently
clears away Grief's daughter,

teardrops.

wiped by your hand,
absorbed into resilience,
we reconnect in the mountains –
planting next year's harvest.

intentions.

change as we evolve
our support as we climb,
whispered under pillowtalk
conferences,

prayer.

culver city

i.

a bike ride
in the late November sun,
where He teaches me
how to trust,
again,
while he remembers
how to fly,
again.

ii.

He:
drinks merrily
from the river Life.
is the heaven who Jesus
was a prophet for
the answer every soul
prays for.

iii.
    He who has found the
    hidden valley lies deep
    within Her safety.
    He has found safety
    and I, peace:
    it starts at the edge
    of my bosom, ending at
    the edge of the universe.

    He's found safety,
    I've found heaven.

chiquita

Us.

a late night thumb war
that lead to something more.

we paint a house
with the love we make
manifesting to God above
that this moment grows
into years,

into more time,
into a life.

**that one summer
we only listened
to frank ocean:**

skyline to

    a prelude to desire:

    come feel the valleys of my stomach,
    roam the fields of my sanctuary &
    taste the strawberry fields
    that are my lips.

    come embrace my being as one;
    to be here
    in your arms
    is to be one with
    God.

sable

within my eyes
resides a galaxy
far beyond your
understanding,

soaring across
space and time,
my ancestors light my
view and align my sight.

deep within my soul
lies a solar system.
held from the gravity
of my Mother
and my Grandmother,
i'm held within love and light.

nestled beneath my bosom,
a fortress
predicated from the support
of my Sistas,

my black body,
my female flight.

i - a mantra

i can turn energy around
in my mind.
i can make you believe
in God
in one drive.

i am powerful.
i am ever changing.
i can bear the wounds
of thousands gracefully.

burbank

chilled, cold fingertips
shuffle through crinkly sheets
to meet my belly –

the moon reflects
from your window pane,
our spotlight. the howling wind
becomes a gentle breeze
as it creeps in
through the small cracks
to greet us in your bed,
our stage.

your chilled, cold fingertips
meander from my belly
to my breasts,
to my heart,
my throat,
my mind
and thighs.

i hum a gleeful tune –
a whispered thank you
as you mold my face
with your eyes.

we stay here like this.

in wind and rain,
dusk and daybreak.

we stay here like this,

strands of intertwining DNA,
sprawled out in sanctuary
as the world rotates forward
with us.
for us.

we stay here,
just like this,
growing, in warmth,
in heat,
in worship,
in sheets.

we stay here like this.

kauai

he saw my aura
as we laid on the bed,
serenaded by roosters
and cicadas.
he glanced around my face,
captured my glow.
his eyes were open,
his heart, full.

"It's yellow."

we held hands on the beach
walking toward the sunset,
chasing the last glimpses of light
and color on my solar return.
we talked of our future,
musing the thought of creating -
a home.

"I could raise a child here..."

wanderlust

we howled,
like the wolves we are,
to the overcasted moon
sitting above us
on the mountain that
we happened upon.
we sang into the
night that tried to silence
our voices.

We are here.

yosemite

we sought refuge in the rocks:
a safe haven in the trees,
underneath the stars.

lost in the valleys,
you found your way back to me.
we climbed a staircase
to heaven and met hell
along the way,
but at the top of the waterfall,
you found your way back to me.

monsoon

to the girl who
brought the rain,
thank you
for the nourishment;
your storm clouds,
cumbersome and slow, surrendered,
blessing this drought riddled soil

with new birth,
new earth,
new breath.

selah

to the girl who
brought the rain,
tempest daughter,
monsoon maven:
your isolated atmospheric
tear drops cleansed
the blight, pardoning
Our mother country's heart center,
Our solar plexus homeland.

your trials are waterfalls

selah

your trials erode eons
of stagnation.
your trials,
an encumbrance,
a storm
breeds resuscitation
to the scarcity that once
threatened this place.

your trials freed
our ancestors,
liberated our mother,
healed our brethren,
and brought you back to me.

selah

thank you for your
steadfast faith:
in me,
your ambrosial reflection
in our future,
our fortitude.

to the girl who brought
the rain, thank you.

thank you
for the salvation of
your gentle smile; for
without its brilliance
as a constant reminder
in every windowpane,
reflective screen,
person we meet,

i surely would have been lost
in the chaos you climbed.

so, to the girl
who brought the rain,

I love you.

I pray for your peace.
I pray for your love.
I pray for your joy.
I pray for your abundance.
I pray for your rest.

selah

epilogue
you are free

to the reader who has
made it this far,
friend, lover, soul partner,
thank you for giving
my ever wild heart,
my ever rampant mind
space and time

to simply *be.*

thank you for taking us
along for your own journey.
every word, every page,
stanza, comma and metaphor
was for you,
or me,
for us,
so we can be
free.
free.
even for a moment,
f r e e .

to be liberated,
exonerated
understood, held
and appreciated
for each silent battle
we fought,
that we fight.
in each silent war
we lost, because there's
still light. each time
we picked ourselves up,
each time our community
and chosen family reached back
to remind us,

we are alive.
we are here.
we matter.
our feelings are valid,
and our journey,
though arduous, glorious.

remember to celebrate:
the smallest of the small
steps forward,
the moments of reprieve
in the storm,
the sunshine;
may she always grant
you warmth, grounding

and love;
the moonlight,
may she always hold space
for your inner dialogue;
your breath,
for it is your
heart's first song;
remember to allow it to be
boisterous,
an uproar,
a battle cry and
your own personal lullaby.

remember, if nothing at all,
please remember,
you are loved.
you are healing.
you are learning.
this is your own personal journey.
don't compare or despair
over what someone else
has or what has yet to come.
you are capable.
you are wild.
you are safe.
you are free.

NOMAD the Poet is an award winning filmmaker, spoken word artist and activist who uses art to raise awareness and consciousness of the human condition. Using art as an educational tool, NOMAD focuses her work to delve into the complexities of healing through trauma for the BIPOC, LGBTQIA+ and people living with disabilities, while also using her art to empower her communities and provide a blueprint for healing, love, validation and self liberation. Her films combine visuals, movement and dance, music, spoken word, and a narrative arc to humanize and actualize the real, raw, and authentic moments, trials, and joys of humanity.

Her work has been featured in the Anthologies:
A Celebration of Young Poets, 2005
People of Paradise, 2017
These Black Bodies: A Chorus of Black Voices, 2023
And has been featured in magazines:
They/Us
Voyage LA

Her experimental shorts films include, *#MelaninRich*, the award winning *The Sable Dragonfly: An Ode to My Black Female Body, Currents*; all can be found online. NOMAD the Poet and her creative team are in the beginning stages of producing a new feature length film, Rebirth, which is expected to be released at the end of 2025.

Fun fact: When NOMAD the Poet is not on the mic, you can find her gleefully flouncing around Los Angeles, jamming to music in the passenger seat of a Subaru Outback. She enjoys running after cats, dogs, chickens, turtles and other furry babies all day long and feeds stray cats anytime she can.

Other Books by Mama's Kitchen Press

If you enjoyed this book, please consider checking out some of our others. Readers like you allow us to keep our kitchen cooking with wonderful books. Thank you!

I'm Writing to Tell You, by Jaha Zainabu

Sown in Light: poetry for the forgotten soul, by Tekira Briscoe

Just Be Honest: a poetic invitation to liberation, by Alexander James

Sorority of Bereaved Mothers: poems and stories from Black Women on pregnancy loss and infertility, Edited by Camari Carter Hawkins

Shooting Stars At Sky: the poetry of play, Edited by Mike Bonifer

Available at www.mamaskitchenpress.com

www.ingramcontent.com/pod-product-compliance
Lightning Source LLC
Chambersburg PA
CBHW051629120626
46551CB00014B/2002